The Short Guide

French
Wines and Champagnes

EDITIONS KACTUS

General Knowledge Friend Companion

This book has been prepared with the greatest care by our teams and we hope that it will give you complete satisfaction.

We would be grateful if you would take the time to write a comment, which we hope will be positive, or to make suggestions for improvements, which we will consult with the greatest interest.

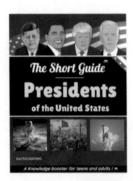
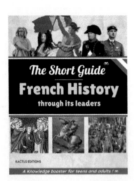
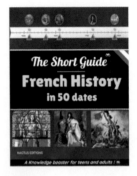

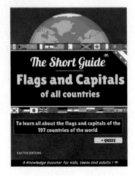
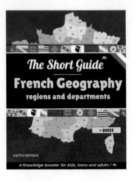

Find us on our Instagram page and follow all our new general knowledge boosters!
(QR code at the back of the book)

Table of contents

How to taste wine or champagne?   P4-5

The stages of winemaking: from the vine to the bottle   P6-7

The different vineyards by region   P8-37

Grape varieties and their aromas   P38-39

Which wine for each dish? The perfect pairing   P40-41

Wine tasting has become an art and it is important to master the basics in order to fully appreciate its aromas and delight the most demanding guests.

First of all, the serving temperature is important, as it influences both the perception of the aromas and the sensation in the mouth. The ideal temperature is specific to each type of wine:

16-18 °C	Deep red wines
14-16 °C	Silky and fruity red wines
11-13 °C	Light red wines, deep white wines, great champagnes
8-11 °C	Rosés, sweet and fruity white wines
6-8 °C	Sparkling wines, champagnes, dry white wines

Beyond the temperature, it is also the order in which the different wines are served that is important. The sequence of flavors must remain pleasant and the tasting of a glass must not make you regret the previous one. Thus, in order not to confuse the taste buds, the tasting is done from the liveliest/lightest to the most powerful and robust wine:

Dry sparkling wine → Dry white wine → Deep white wine / Light red wine → Deep red wine → Sweet wine

Moreover, it is better to taste an old wine before a young one in order to better appreciate its finesse.

Finally, wines can also be aerated before tasting (poured into a carafe). Although there is no absolute rule on this, airing the wine will bring out the full range of aromas. However, for an old wine, exposure to the open air can also alter the taste. Therefore, this process is preferable for young wines. The duration of aeration differs again according to the age, type and quality of the wine, with aeration of 2 hours for classic wines and 3 hours for exceptional wines.

Now that you have mastered the first precepts and the main mistakes to avoid, let's move on to wine tasting itself. This is simpler than it seems: trust your senses.

Sight

The first step to properly tasting a wine is to contemplate it. This allows you to potentially guess the grape varieties or the location of the wine.

The **color** is also interesting to determine the probable age of the wine you are tasting: white wine reflections are first green then silver (usually two years old) then gold and finally bronze. Red wine is more cherry at first, then more and more tile.

Finally, you can observe the **wine's tears**, the traces left by the wine on the edge of the glass when you tilt it. This will allow you to determine the presence of sugars in the wine, particularly wise in the case of white wines.

Smell

Let's move on to the sense of smell, which includes two stages: the first nose and the second nose.

First nose: Without aerating it, it allows to recognize the defects of the wine ("cork taste" for example), the aromas being still not very developed.

Second nose: After aeration, it allows to distinguish the 3 types of aromas. The primary aromas which come from the grape variety and the floral environment of the vineyard, the secondary aromas linked to the fermentation and the tertiary aromas which come from the maturation of the wine.

Taste

Finally, the third and last step is the taste test of the wine. Let the liquid enter your mouth and swirl it around: acidity, sweetness and bitterness are not perceived in the same places in your mouth. You must then pay particular attention to three phases.

First, *the attack*, the first taste in the mouth, determines the power of a wine. Then, *the mid-palate* allows you to feel the flavors. You will be able to feel the acidity of the white wine or the tannins of the red wines. Finally, *the finish* is the evolution of the flavors in the mouth. Even once swallowed, a great wine continues to reveal flavors.

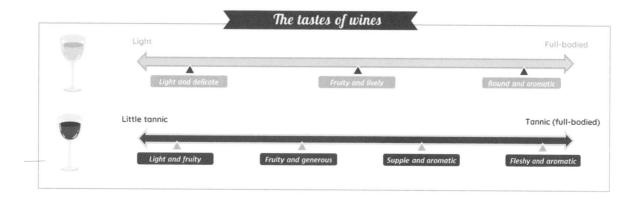

The tastes of wines

Light — Full-bodied
Light and delicate | Fruity and lively | Round and aromatic

Little tannic — Tannic (full-bodied)
Light and fruity | Fruity and generous | Supple and aromatic | Fleshy and aromatic

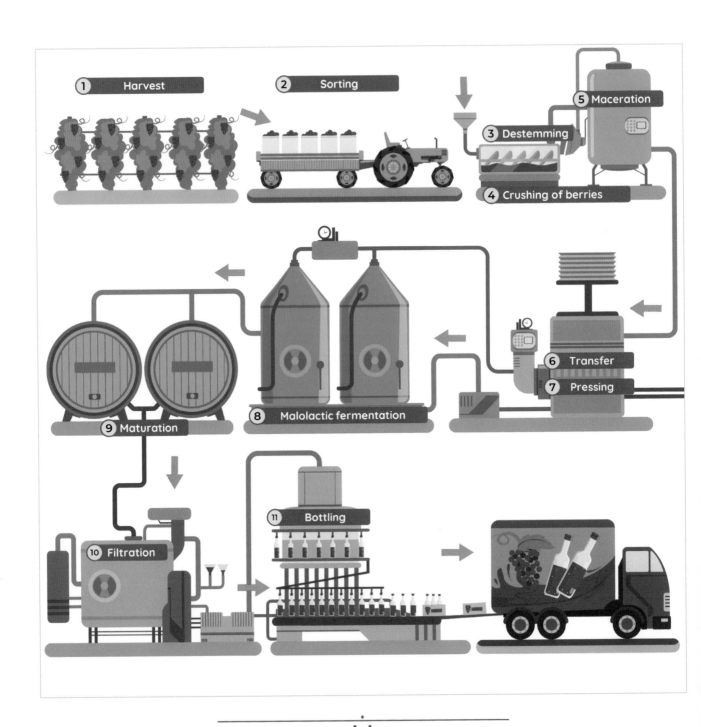

The stages of winemaking: from the vine to the bottle

Winemaking is the process of transforming grapes into a specific type of wine. Like the land on which the vine grows, winemaking is the result of centuries of hard work to produce wines. The different stages of this process differ according to the type of wine (red, white, rosé, champagne, etc.) and each winegrower mixes his tricks to obtain a unique wine. Here is a summary of the 11 stages of French red wine vinification:

1 Harvest It is the harvest of the precious grape. The time of harvesting varies according to the region, but it generally takes place between July and October, depending on the degree of ripeness desired by the winegrower.

2 Sorting The harvested grapes are sorted in order to keep only those corresponding to the needs of the winegrower.

3 Destemming It consists in removing the stalks of the bunch, i.e. the vegetal part. The objective? It is to keep only the grape berries and thus eliminate any risk of bringing bitter tastes to the wine.

4 Crushing The grape berries are crushed to obtain a single liquid: the grape must.

5 Maceration The skin of the grape macerates in the juice for a period of 4 days to 1 month. It is the skin that gives the color to the red wine. Then, the wine ferments.

6 Transfer After a first fermentation, the juice (also called free-run wine), is sent directly into a second large vat while the skin and seeds remaining at the bottom are retrieved.

7 Pressing The recovered seeds are then sent to the press. This pressing will then give the press wine.

8 Malolactic fermentation The press wine is most often reintegrated into the free-run wine and the liquid obtained undergoes a second fermentation called malolactic. The acidity disappears little by little.

9 Maturation The wine is then stored in barrels for up to 3 seasons so that it can release all its aromas.

10 Filtration The wine passes through a filtering machine that removes its roughness and makes it clearer.

11 Bottling The liquid is finally bottled and ready to be distributed worldwide!

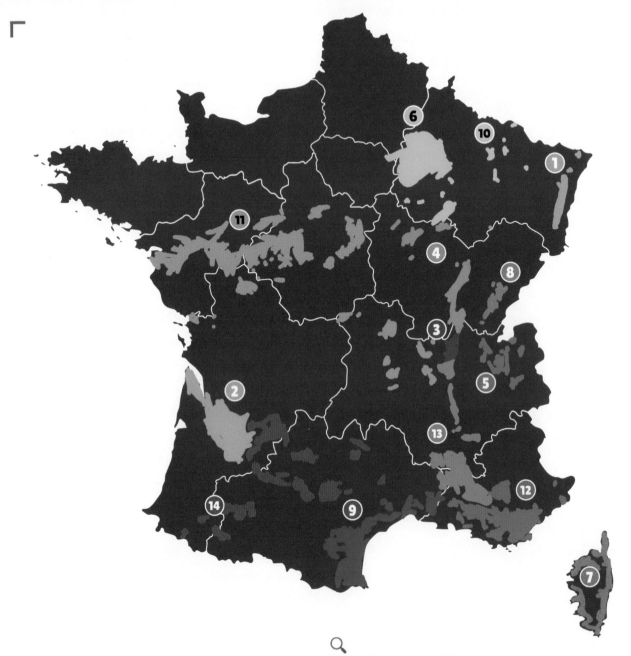

The 14 wine-growing regions

1. Alsace
2. Bordeaux
3. Beaujolais
4. Bourgogne
5. Savoie-Bugey
6. Champagne
7. Corsica
8. Jura
9. Languedoc-Roussillon
10. Lorraine
11. Loire
12. Provence
13. Rhône
14. Sud-Ouest

France has long since acquired the status of "Wine Country" due to the great diversity of its regions and landscapes. With climates particularly conducive to the cultivation of the vine, wine is a true institution in the national culture. In spite of a slight decrease in its consumption over the last few decades, the country keeps a solid second place in the ranking of the largest world producers, just behind Italy with 4.2 billion liters.

| 835 505 hectares | 16 wine regions | 80 departments | 3 240 different wines |

The terroirs combined with a historical know-how have contributed to the worldwide fame of French vineyards, with several exceptional regions: Burgundy, Bordeaux, Champagne, Rhône, etc. Several legendary wines such as Pétrus, Romanée-Conti or Cheval-Blanc can fetch huge sums and are particularly prized by the world's great fortunes.

There are **several labels** at the French and European level to protect the know-how of producers and to guarantee quality to consumers. Since the 2009 reform, there are now 3 types of labels, from the strictest to the least strict:

> **Greatest vintages of French wines: ★ ★ ★ ★ ★**
> Memorable vintages are rarely common to all regions. However, 1945, 1947, 1961, 1989 and 2005 can be mentioned.

○ **Protected Designation of Origin (AOP in french)** formerly *AOC*: It is the most famous of the French appellations. It defends the regional typicity of wines and ensures continuity in viticultural and oenological practices, in accordance with local customs (the grape varieties that can be used, but also the yields). It is the most demanding appellation, although this quality is not necessarily present. Within the AOP, some wines are entitled to the Cru label, a guarantee of quality. This hierarchy varies according to the region.

Grand Cru > Premier Cru > Deuxième Cru > Troisième Cru > Etc...

○ **Protected Geographical Indication (IGP in french)** formerly *Vins de Pays*: the PGI is subject to less restrictive specifications than the PDO. The geographical area is larger and the methods of vine growing and wine making are less fixed.

○ **The Vins De France** formerly *Vins de Table*: Any wine produced in France that does not have a Protected Designation of Origin (PDO, the former AOC) or a Protected Geographical Indication (PGI) is by definition a VDF.

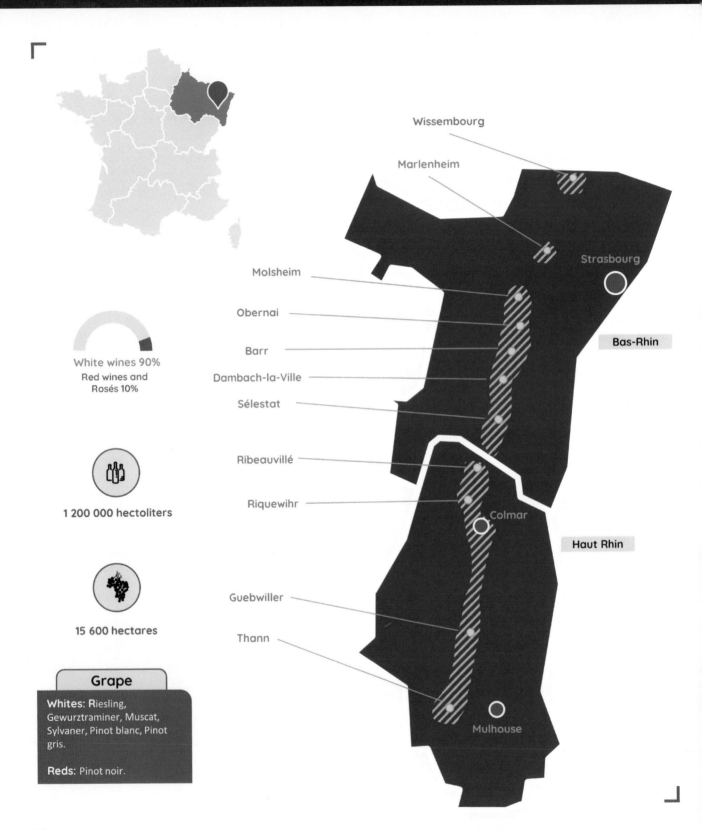

White wines 90%
Red wines and
Rosés 10%

1 200 000 hectoliters

15 600 hectares

Grape

Whites: Riesling,
Gewurztraminer, Muscat,
Sylvaner, Pinot blanc, Pinot
gris.

Reds: Pinot noir.

Wissembourg

Marlenheim

Molsheim

Obernai

Barr

Dambach-la-Ville

Sélestat

Ribeauvillé

Riquewihr

Guebwiller

Thann

Strasbourg

Bas-Rhin

Colmar

Haut Rhin

Mulhouse

At the foot of the Vosges mountains, Alsace benefits from a microclimate that is both humid (600 mm of water per year) and sunny (1800 hours of sunshine per year), which is favorable to vine growing.

In a territory extending from the north of Strasbourg to Mulhouse more in the south, Alsace has built up an excellent reputation for its white wines, whose slender bottles also known as "flutes", are easily recognizable.

Alsatian vineyard (Sélestat)

Characteristic "flute" bottle

Good Alsatian white wines are generally among the fruitiest of French wines. White wines represent 90% of the Alsatian wine production, but there are also several red wines under the appellation Alsace Pinot noir. Moreover, there are 3 wine appellations for the Alsatian vineyard: Alsace Grand Cru, Alsace, Crémant d'Alsace.

Greatest vintages of Alsatian wines:
1929, 1937, 1945, 1947, 1949, 1953, 1955, 1959, 1961, 1964, 1969, 1971, 1976, 1981, 1983, 1985, 1988, 1990, 2000 and 2007.

Our selection

€	€€	€€€
Riesling Domaine Schlumberger	Famille Hugel Gewurztraminer Alsatian white wine	Domaine Deiss Gewurztraminer Late harvest
Grape variety: Riesling **Taste**: Dry, fruity	**Grape variety**: Gewurztraminer **Taste**: Dry, fruity	**Grape variety**: Gewurztraminer **Taste**: Dry, fruity

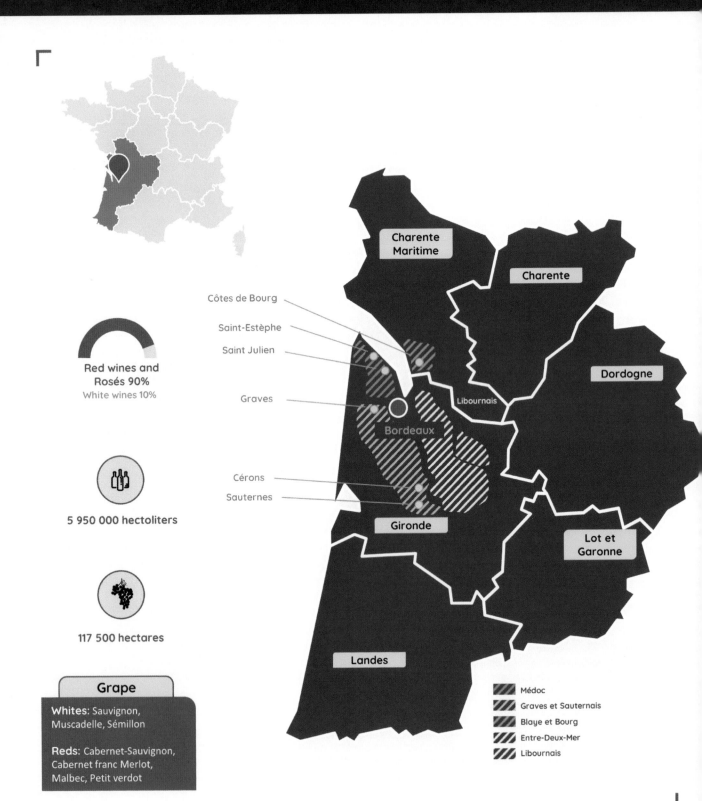

Red wines and
Rosés 90%
White wines 10%

5 950 000 hectoliters

117 500 hectares

Grape

Whites: Sauvignon,
Muscadelle, Sémillon

Reds: Cabernet-Sauvignon,
Cabernet franc Merlot,
Malbec, Petit verdot

Côtes de Bourg
Saint-Estèphe
Saint Julien
Graves
Cérons
Sauternes

Charente
Maritime
Charente
Dordogne
Libournais
Bordeaux
Gironde
Lot et
Garonne
Landes

Médoc
Graves et Sauternais
Blaye et Bourg
Entre-Deux-Mer
Libournais

The reputation of the Bordeaux vineyards is well established: from ancient times to the present day, the land of Bordeaux and its craftsmen have produced wines of rare quality that have made this wine region shine in the eyes of the world. It is therefore quite natural that they are found in the greatest restaurants to accompany the best dishes.

Situated between Gironde and Dordogne rivers, this region with its temperate and oceanic climate is not only suitable for vine growing, but has also managed to excel in its know-how: the Bordeaux style of wine maturing, a stage prior to bottling, gives the wine its particular aromas and a great capacity for conservation.

Maturation of Bordeaux wine in oak barrels (12-18 months)

Bordeaux vineyards (Saint-Emilion)

With its 8,650 chateaux, including the famous Pétrus, Cheval Blanc, Yquem, Latour, Cheval Blanc and Mouton Rothschild, the Bordeaux vineyards have no less than 40 PDO and 2 PGI appellations. The red wines produced here are the finest and rarest in France and the world.

★ ★ ★ ★ ★

Greatest vintages of Bordeaux wines:

1900, 1929, 1949, 1961, 1982, 1990, 2000, 2005, 2009, 2010, 2015 and 2016.

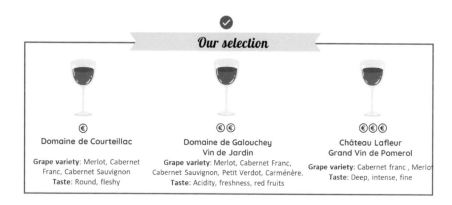

Our selection

€
Domaine de Courteillac

Grape variety: Merlot, Cabernet Franc, Cabernet Sauvignon
Taste: Round, fleshy

€€
Domaine de Galouchey
Vin de Jardin

Grape variety: Merlot, Cabernet Franc, Cabernet Sauvignon, Petit Verdot, Carménère.
Taste: Acidity, freshness, red fruits

€€€
Château Lafleur
Grand Vin de Pomerol

Grape variety: Cabernet franc , Merlot
Taste: Deep, intense, fine

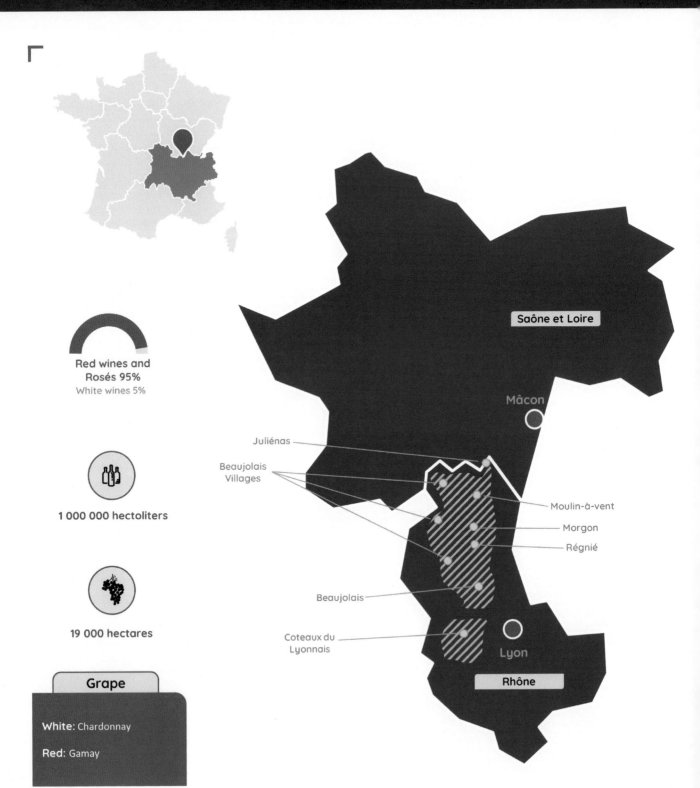

Red wines and
Rosés 95%
White wines 5%

1 000 000 hectoliters

19 000 hectares

Grape

White: Chardonnay

Red: Gamay

Saône et Loire

Mâcon

Juliénas

Beaujolais
Villages

Moulin-à-vent

Morgon

Régnié

Beaujolais

Coteaux du
Lyonnais

Lyon

Rhône

The Beaujolais region is an unfailing vineyard of Lyon's culinary culture and is mainly known for its Beaujolais Nouveau, an early wine bottled after vinification. This wine of the year, generally tasted with Lyon's delicatessen, has not really enjoyed a great reputation compared to its competitors from Bordeaux or Burgundy, but it has managed to establish itself in the popular culture. It is the wine merchant and ace communicator Georges Dubœuf who was able to put Beaujolais nouveau on the front of the stage, both nationally and internationally, by rallying to its annual launch (in November) many winemakers and restaurateurs in the region.

For the past few years, however, some Beaujolais wines have been inviting themselves onto large tables with fruity notes and capable of aging for 10 years or more.

Beaujolais nouveau celebrated in Tokyo in November 2017

Beaujolais vineyard (Juliénas)

With its 3000 chateaux and estates, the Beaujolais vineyard has 12 PDO wine appellations and 2 PGI appellations. The red wines produced here are generally fruity and not very tannic. The white wines, which are produced in small quantities and based on Chardonnay, are usually dry.

★ ★ ★ ★ ★

Greatest vintages of Beaujolais wines:

1949, 1952, 1959, 1961, 1966, 1969, 1971, 1976, 2005, 2009 and 2011.

Our selection

€	€€	€€€
Beaujolais villages Château du Chatelard	Morgon Daniel Bouland Les Delys	Morgon Jean Foillard Athenor
Grape variety: Gamay **Taste:** Light, fruity	**Grape variety:** Gamay **Taste:** Fruity, fleshy	**Grape variety:** Gamay **Taste:** Fruity, fleshy

White and sparkling wines 70%

Red wines 30%

1 450 000 hectoliters

29 500 hectares

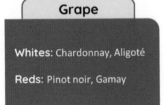

Grape

Whites: Chardonnay, Aligoté

Reds: Pinot noir, Gamay

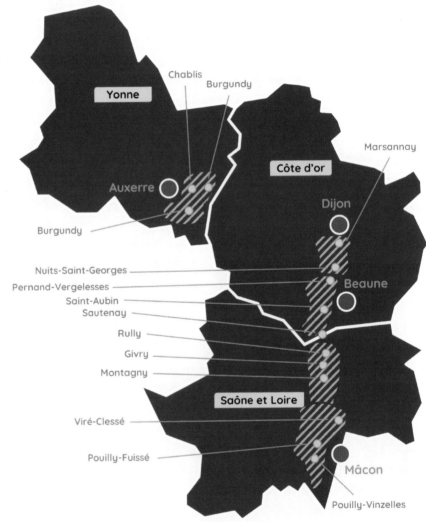

Yonne

Chablis

Burgundy

Côte d'or

Marsannay

Auxerre

Dijon

Burgundy

Nuits-Saint-Georges

Pernand-Vergelesses

Saint-Aubin

Sautenay

Beaune

Rully

Givry

Montagny

Saône et Loire

Viré-Clessé

Pouilly-Fuissé

Mâcon

Pouilly-Vinzelles

In the 14th century, the Duke of Burgundy Philippe le Hardi ordered the planting of Gamay on his lands, which he did not find noble enough, in favor of Pinot Noir, which was much better adapted to the climate. What a great decision for his region and for our taste buds! Since then, the region produces some of the best red wines in the world.

But Burgundy's wine production does not stop at red wine. Indeed, the white and sparkling wine, mainly from Chardonnay, represents 70% of this production and participates in the worldwide fame of the region.

Romanée-Conti, Jean-François Coche Dury, Mortet and many other domains produce bottles that are sold at premium prices. Fortunately, there are many domains that produce excellent and more affordable wines

Hospices de Beaune

1945 bottle of Romanée-Conti sold at auction for $588,000 in 2018

The Mâconnais, the Côte Chalonnaise, the Côte de Beaune, the Côte de Nuits, the Chablis or the Grand Auxerrois: there are no less than 4,000 estates (the Hospices de Beaune in particular), 83 AOP appellations and 5 IGP appellations throughout these sub-regions. The white wines are generally dry and the reds fine.

★ ★ ★ ★ ★

Greatest vintages of Burgundy wines:

1929, 1934, 1945, 1947, 1961, 1969, 1986, 1996, 1999, and 2009.

Our selection

Bourgogne Chardonnay Closerie des Alisiers	Château des Rontets "Bourgogne du Sud" dry white	Domaine Chavy-Chouet Pommard 1er Cru
(€)	(€)(€)	(€)(€)(€)
Grape variety: Chardonnay	**Grape variety:** Chardonnay	**Grape variety:** Pinot noir
Taste: Fresh, dry	**Taste:** Fresh, airy	**Taste:** Deep, intense

Wines of Savoie Bugey

Red wines 61 %

Whites and sparkling wines
31 %

166 000 hectoliters

5 770 hectares

Grape

Whites: Chardonnay, Jacquère, Roussanne, Altesse, Chasselas et Molette
Reds: Poulsard, Mondeuse, Pinot noir et Gamay

Cerdon
Seyssel
Crépy
Marin
Bonneville

Ain
Bourg-en-Bresse
Annecy
Haute-Savoie
Lagnieu
Chambéry
Savoie
Grenoble
Belley
Apremont
Monthoux
Isère
Les Abymes

Bugey
Savoie

This small vineyard nestled in the French Pre-Alps manages to seduce even the greatest tables in the world with its wines of varied aromas. This small wine-producing territory, with its wide variety of climates and grape varieties, also bears a heavy past.

In 1248, the collapse of Mount Granier wiped out the vineyard, whose origins date back to the Roman occupation during the Antiquity. This landslide ravaged an area of more than 25km², leaving nothing to this mountain vineyard, which the inhabitants considered cursed.

In the 18th century, small craftsmen and peasants gradually restored the letters of nobility of this vineyard nestled on the heights. The production reaches today 166 000 hectoliters.

Savoyard vineyards in terraces (Lake Geneva shores)

Apremont, Abymes, the wines of Savoie have been increasingly successful for several decades and have taken the wines of Bugey in their wake. The region now has no less than 5 PDO and 4 PGI appellations. These bottles will offer full satisfaction, especially around a good raclette or fondue savoyarde!

★★★★★

Greatest vintages of Savoie Bugey wines:

1988, 1990, 1985, 2002 and 2005.

Our selection

€
Savoie Apremont
Rémy Berlioz
Grape variety: Jacquère
Taste: Dry, fruity

€€
Roussette de Savoie
Domaine Jean Perrier et fils
Grape variety: Altesse
Taste: Round, fruity

€€€
Allobrogie
Domaine des Ardoisières
Grape variety: Mondeuse noire, Persan
Taste: Deep, fine

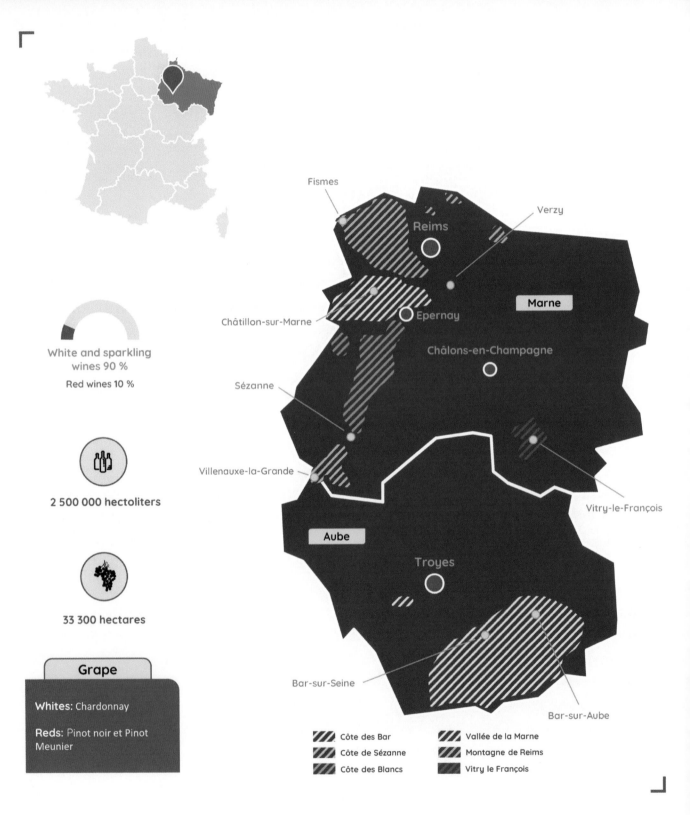

White and sparkling
wines 90 %

Red wines 10 %

2 500 000 hectoliters

33 300 hectares

Grape

Whites: Chardonnay

Reds: Pinot noir et Pinot Meunier

Fismes

Reims

Verzy

Châtillon-sur-Marne

Epernay

Marne

Châlons-en-Champagne

Sézanne

Villenauxe-la-Grande

Vitry-le-François

Aube

Troyes

Bar-sur-Seine

Bar-sur-Aube

Côte des Bar

Côte de Sézanne

Côte des Blancs

Vallée de la Marne

Montagne de Reims

Vitry le François

Champagne is one of the most renowned wine regions in the world. A name that rhymes with celebration and refinement. In the 17th century, the Benedictine monk Dom Pérignon created this sparkling wine and the famous Champagne method to obtain it: the addition of the liqueur de tirage (sugar, yeast and old wine) to a mixture of several still wines (not sparkling) previously fermented. This process produces carbon dioxide and therefore bubbles when the bottle is opened.

Moët et Chandon, Dom Pérignon, Ruinart, Veuve Clicquot,... the list of the great Champagne houses that have seduced the whole world is long, but the secret lies especially in their judicious blending. The marriage between wines of different grape varieties, plots, years and aromatic qualities offers bottles of exceptional quality, declined under several types:

Brut Champagne	Vintage Brut Champagne	Semi-Dry Champagne	Blanc de Noir Champagne	Blanc de Blanc Champagne	Rosé Champagne
Champagne of reference - low sugar content	Made of wines from the same year - allows to highlight exceptional vintages	Higher sugar content - recommended for dessert	Made only from black grapes with white flesh (Pinot noir and Pinot Meunier) - powerful and aromatic champagnes	Made only from white grapes (Chardonnay) - fresh and delicate champagne produced mainly on the mountain of Reims	Elaborated by combining white and red wine

This wine territory is divided into 6 regions (Côte des blancs, Côte des Bar, Côte de Sézanne, Vallée de la Marne, Montagne de Reims and Vitry-le-François) producing mainly this famous sparkling wine. The appellation "Champagne" is exclusive to the vineyard. Crémant, sparkling wine or prosecco, although sparkling, cannot use this name.

★ ★ ★ ★ ★

Greatest vintages of Champagnes:

1900, 1911, 1914, 1921, 1937, 1955, 1975, 1990, 1996 and 2002

Our selection

€
Champagne Bonnaire Tradition L'Esprit du Temps
Grape variety: Chardonnay, Pinot Noir, Pinot Meunier
Taste: Spicy, fruity

€€
Champagne Bonnaire "Variance" (Blanc de Blancs sous bois)
Grape variety: Chardonnay
Taste: Candied fruits, vanilla

€€€
Champagne Billecart Salmon « Blanc de Blanc Grand Cru »
Grape variety: Chardonnay
Taste: Floral, brioche

Red wines and Rosés 85 %

White wines 15 %

98 000 hectoliters

7 180 hectares

Grape

Whites: Vermentino, Muscat à petits grains

Reds: Nielluccio, Sciaccarello, Grenache

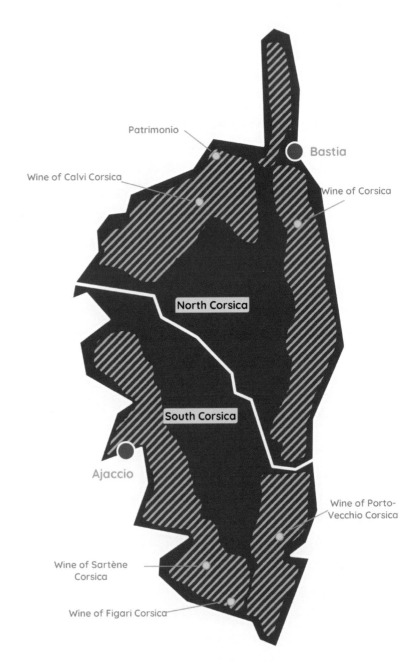

Patrimonio

Bastia

Wine of Calvi Corsica

Wine of Corsica

North Corsica

South Corsica

Ajaccio

Wine of Porto-Vecchio Corsica

Wine of Sartène Corsica

Wine of Figari Corsica

Historical vineyard whose origins go back to more than 2500 years, the Corsican wine has however rather recently known a difficult period. During the 20th century, the production increased strongly to fill the growing demand in France. But this increase was at the expense of quality: Corsican wine progressively lost its identity, its character and even its territory.

Since the 80's, the vineyard has been recovering its colors on the Island of Beauty with grape varieties such as the Vermentino. The culture of the vineyard is taking back the territory and the craftsmen propose today white wines with floral flavors and colored and powerful red wines.

Corsica vineyard

Vermentino grape variety

Because of their geological similarities, the Corsican vineyard is often linked to the vineyard of Provence. However, thanks to the hard work of its producers, Corsican wine is asserting itself as a wine-producing territory in its own right.

★ ★ ★ ★ ★

Greatest vintages of Corsican wines:

1988, 1989, 1990, 1998, 2000, 2006 and 2007.

Our selection

€
Ile de Beauté
Domaine Casanova
Grape variety: Sciacarellu, Cinsault
Taste: Fruity

€€
Ile de Beauté
Domaine Saint Armettu - Mino
Grape variety: Niellucciu, Sciaccarellu, Syrah
Taste: Fleshy, fruity

€€€
Ile de Beauté
Domaine Sant Armettu - Burghese
Grape variety: Vermentinu, Genovese, Biancu ghjentile
Taste: Firm, fleshy

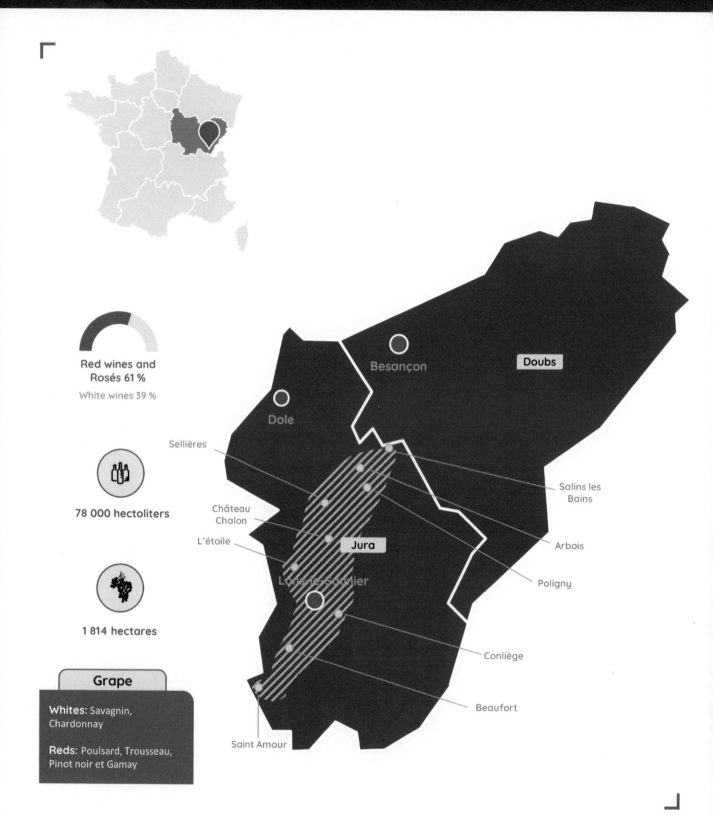

Red wines and Rosés 61 %

White wines 39 %

78 000 hectoliters

1 814 hectares

Grape

Whites: Savagnin, Chardonnay

Reds: Poulsard, Trousseau, Pinot noir et Gamay

Besançon

Doubs

Dole

Sellières

Salins les Bains

Château Chalon

L'étoile

Jura

Arbois

Poligny

Lons-le-Saunier

Conliège

Beaufort

Saint Amour

Small in area but with a recognized wealth of wine production, the Jura vineyards stretch over an 80km long and 6km wide strip, from Salins-les-Bains to Saint-Amour. The small farms and cooperatives that make up the vineyard produce a wide variety of wines.

Between vigorous red wines and more classic white wines based on Chardonnay, there is the excellent yellow wine du Jura: obtained thanks to the Savagnin grape variety and a specific method of maturing which makes it very solid and suitable for longer storage, yellow wine is characterized by its nutty taste. It is the ideal wine to taste with Comté cheese or poularde de Bresse. It is easily recognizable by its container (the clavelin) with its particular shape.

Clavelin (62 cl) reserved for yellow wine

Vat of yellow wine maturing (6 years and 3 months in total)

Moreover, this territory is also the home of the famous straw wine, sweet and rich in aromas, which goes perfectly with the local specialties. These ancient expertises in this small area make the Jura one of the most surprising wine regions in France!

★ ★ ★ ★ ★

Greatest vintages of Jura wines:

1988,1990,1985, 2002 and 2005.

Our selection

€

Domaine Tissot Arbois Chardonnay "Patchwork"

Grape variety: Chardonnay
Taste: Dry, fruity

€ €

Arbois yellow wine Domaine badoz

Grape variety: Savagnin
Taste: Smooth, nutty

€ € €

Arbois yellow wine Caveau de Bacchus

Grape variety: Savagnin
Taste: Refined, smooth

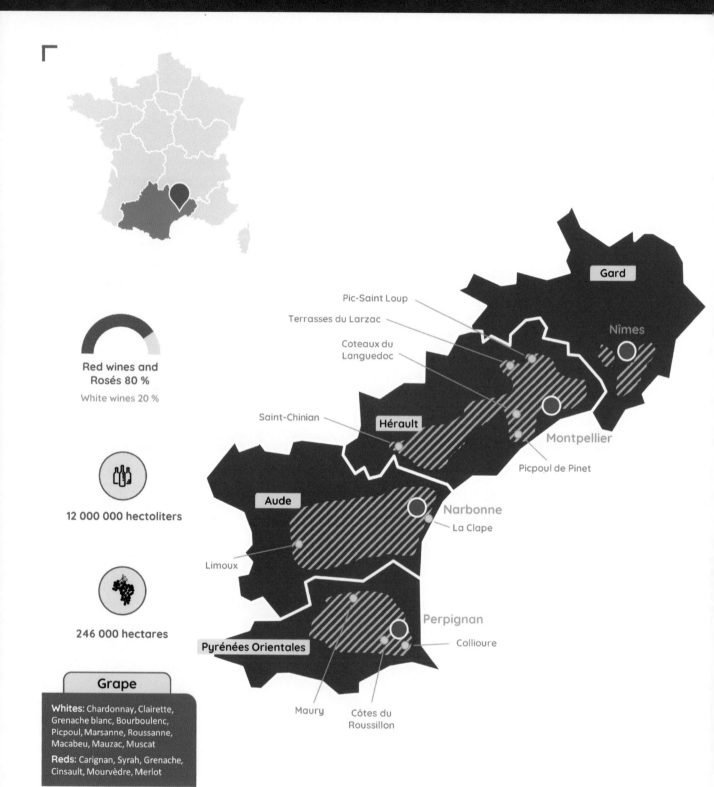

Red wines and
Rosés 80 %

White wines 20 %

12 000 000 hectoliters

246 000 hectares

Grape

Whites: Chardonnay, Clairette, Grenache blanc, Bourboulenc, Picpoul, Marsanne, Roussanne, Macabeu, Mauzac, Muscat

Reds: Carignan, Syrah, Grenache, Cinsault, Mourvèdre, Merlot

Gard

Nîmes

Pic-Saint Loup

Terrasses du Larzac

Coteaux du
Languedoc

Hérault

Montpellier

Saint-Chinian

Picpoul de Pinet

Aude

Narbonne

La Clape

Limoux

Perpignan

Pyrénées Orientales

Collioure

Maury

Côtes du
Roussillon

The Languedoc-Roussillon vineyard is the largest wine-producing area in France and the top producer in France. Spread over four departments (Pyrénées Orientales, Aude, Hérault and Gard), vines have been cultivated here since antiquity and the Greco-Roman invasions.

The wines produced from a large number of grape varieties offer a very wide range of aromas and are becoming increasingly popular with consumers. Indeed, for the past few years, artisans have made it a point of honor to offer quality wines: Canet Valette, Gauby, La Grange des Pères,... Languedoc-Roussillon wines are now being served on the best tables. Although prices are gradually increasing, very good deals are still possible!

Syrah grape variety offering powerful red wines

Vineyards on the Terrasses du Larzac

Long compared to the wines of the Rhone Valley, the wines of Languedoc-Roussillon stand out in particular thanks to the terraces of Larzac which constitute a true territory of wine innovation where many neo-winegrowers offer stunning bottles!

★★★★★

Greatest vintages of Languedoc-Roussillon wines:

1990, 1991, 1995, 1998, 2001, 2003, 2004, 2005, 2006 and 2010.

Our selection

€

Languedoc
Les Darons by Jeff Carrel
Grape variety: Grenache, Carignan, Syrah
Taste: Dry, fruity

€€

Pays d'Oc
Chemin de Moscou - Domaine Gayda
Grape variety: Syrah, Grenache, Cinsault.
Taste: Spicy, mineral

€€€

Terrasses du Larzac – Domaine de la Peira en Damaisela
Grape variety: Syrah, Grenache
Taste: Fleshy, powerful

Red and grey
wines 95 %

White wines 5 %

13 800 hectoliters

180 hectares

Grape

Whites: Auxerrois, Chardonnay

Reds: Pinot noir, Gamay

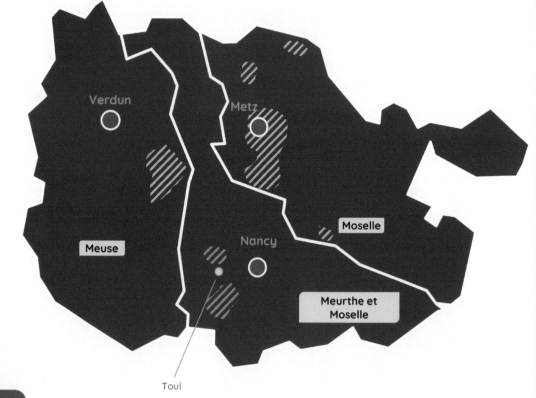

Verdun

Metz

Moselle

Nancy

Meuse

Meurthe et
Moselle

Toul

 Moselle
 Meuse
Toul

A historic and formerly prolific vineyard, Lorraine was hard hit by the successive confrontations of the 19th and 20th centuries, with its surface area falling from 34,000 hectares in 1840 to 180 today.

Lorraine is known for its grey wine "onion skin", a rosé wine with a light color. Produced from grapes with black skin and white flesh, the grey wine has the particularity to result from a direct pressing, with a very short maceration time (only a few hours). The must, i.e. the grape juice, has very little contact with the skin of the grape, which explains its lightly colored appearance. Gris-de-Toul is known for its fruity taste.

Lorraine vineyard (Côtes de Toul)

Lorrain grey wine

The region also produces white wines close to the Alsatian style and is on a positive dynamic attracting many young winemakers who are busy restoring Lorraine to its former glory.

★ ★ ★ ★ ★

Greatest vintages of Lorraine wines:

1921, 1918, 1945, 1961, 1983, 1990 and 2000.

Our selection

€

Côtes de Toul grey wine
Grape variety: Gamay, Pinot noir
Tasty: Fruity, flowery

€€

Auxerrois Côtes de Toul La Chaponnière
Grape variety: Gamay, Pinot noir
Taste: Fruity, flowery, supple

White wines 55 %

Red wines and
Rosés 45 %

3 175 00 hectoliters

70 000 hectares

Grape

Whites: Melon de
Bourgogne, Chenin,
Sauvignon, Chardonnay

Reds: Cabernet franc,
Gamay, Pinot noir

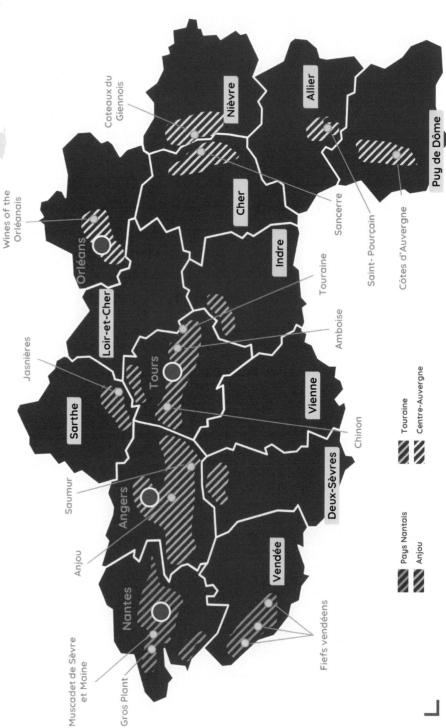

Coteaux du Giennois

Nièvre

Allier

Puy de Dôme

Wines of the Orléanais

Orléans

Cher

Sancerre

Saint-Pourçain

Côtes d'Auvergne

Indre

Touraine

Amboise

Loir-et-Cher

Jasnières

Tours

Vienne

Chinon

Sarthe

Saumur

Angers

Anjou

Deux-Sèvres

Vendée

Fiefs vendéens

Nantes

Muscadet de Sèvre et Maine

Gros Plant

Touraine

Centre-Auvergne

Pays Nantais

Anjou

The Loire vineyard is the most extensive wine region in France, covering more than 1000 km² along the river, from its estuary near Nantes to the Massif Central. The wines produced there, of a rare finesse and great variety (red, rosé and dry white, sparkling, sweet..) have long contributed to France's reputation in this field.

Beyond its gustatory and aromatic quality, the Loire vineyards are distinguished by their visual beauty: the vines are grown along the great castles of the Loire, to the delight of wine tourists who can admire these marvels of French architecture while tasting Loire wines.

Vineyard of the Loire

There are 5 main regions for Loire wines: Nantais, particularly known for its Muscadet (dry and acidic white wine); Anjou-Saumurois and Touraine, which offer a wide variety of wines, including Chenin-based whites and Cabernet Franc reds (easy to drink and often offered in Parisian bistros); Centre-Val de Loire, the land of Sauvignon; Auvergne, known for its light, fruity wine, produced in particular at Saint-Pourçain-sur-Sioule.

★ ★ ★ ★ ★

Greatest vintages of Loire wines:

1906, 1911, 1919, 1921, 1929, 1945, 1947, 1959, 1971, 1989, 1995, 1996, 1997, 2001 and 2007.

Our selection

€
Sauvignon Tourraine Chateau de Vallagon
Grape variety: Sauvignon
Taste: Dry, fruity

€€
Bourgueil - Domaine Yannick Amirault La petite cave
Grape variety: Cabernet-franc
Taste: Fleshy, fruity

€€€
Coulée de Serrant
Grape variety: Chenin
Taste: Supple, fruity

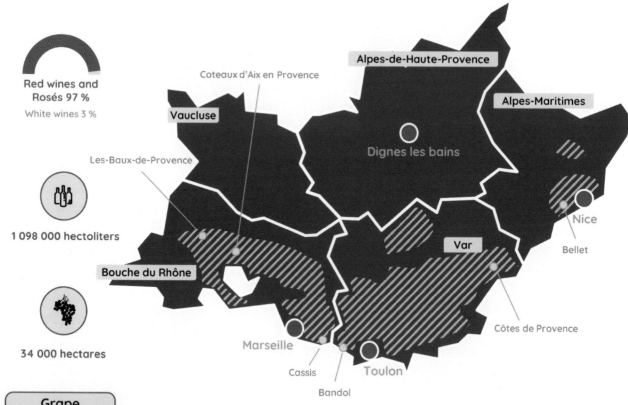

Red wines and
Rosés 97 %

White wines 3 %

1 098 000 hectoliters

34 000 hectares

Coteaux d'Aix en Provence

Alpes-de-Haute-Provence

Alpes-Maritimes

Vaucluse

Dignes les bains

Les-Baux-de-Provence

Nice

Bellet

Var

Bouche du Rhône

Côtes de Provence

Marseille

Cassis

Toulon

Bandol

Grape

Whites: Rolle (Vermentino),
Grenache blanc, Clairette,
Bourboulenc, Ugni blanc

Reds: Carignan, Syrah,
Grenache, Cinsault, Mourvèdre,
Tibouren, Folle noire

Provence is the ancient cradle of French viticulture and is a region known for its rosés (produced in large quantities, representing 85% of its production), its reds and its whites. With a region that rhymes with vacations, sun and olive trees, Provence rosé wines are a huge success during the summer and cover no less than 40% of the French demand in this area. However, this success tends to mask the excellent crystal clear white wines or the complex reds (Bandol) of the region's talented winegrowers.

The vineyards of Provence stretch from south of Avignon to Nice, covering most of Provence. Geologically close, Provence is often associated with Corsica for their viticultural similarities.

Vineyard of Provence

Bottles " flute with corset " (left) and " Côte-de-Provence " (right)

There are two types of bottles for the Côtes de Provence appellation: the "flute bottle" (narrow base) for the wines of the owners, and the "Côte-de-Provence" bottle used by merchants. Nevertheless, most often it is the more popular Bordeaux shape that is used by most producers in the region.

★ ★ ★ ★ ★

Greatest vintages of Loire wines:

1988, 1989, 1990, 1998, 2000, 2006 and 2007.

Our selection

Côtes de Provence - Maîtres Vignerons de Vidauban	Côtes de Provence - Cuvée Rose et Or Château Minuty	Bandol - Domaine de la Begude - La Brûlade
€	€€	€€€
Grape variety: Grenache, Carignan, Cinsault, Syrah, Mourvèdre	**Grape variety:** Grenache, Syrah	**Grape variety:** Mourvèdre, Grenache noir
Taste: Fruity	**Taste:** Fruity	**Taste:** Deep, fine, fruity

Red wines and Rosés 90 %

White wines 10 %

2 830 000 hectoliters

73 800 hectares

Grape

Whites: Viognier, Marsanne, Roussanne, Clairette, Bourboulenc, Picpoul, Grenache blanc, Ugni blanc.

Reds: Syrah, Grenache, Mourvèdre, Carignan, Cinsault, Counoise, Vaccarèse

Rhône

Condrieu

Loire

Lyon

Isère

Hermitage

Saint-Péray

Valence

Clairette de Die

Ardèche

Drôme

Côtes du Rhône village

Lirac

Vinsobres

Costières de Nîmes

Châteauneuf-du-Pape

Nîmes

Gard

Avignon

Vaucluse

▨ Rhône septentrional
▨ Rhône méridional

The vineyards of the Rhone Valley have an impressive geological variety offering land suitable for the cultivation of a large number of grape varieties and allowing the production of very elaborate wines (the red wine Châteauneuf-du-pape is made from 13 different grape varieties). This region, which is very well known today for the quality of its wines, has its origins in ancient times when the Romans built the first terraced vineyards.

There are two main wine regions in the Rhone Valley: the Northern Rhone, from the south of Lyon to the north of Valence (mainly known for its powerful red wines) and the Southern Rhone, from the south of Valence to Avignon, known for its very sophisticated wines.

Rhone vineyards in terraces

These Rhone wines, which can excel in quality (Condrieu or Chateau Grillet in the north are white wines renowned for their aromatic richness) can also be treacherous. It is not uncommon for the alcohol concentration of certain cheap bottles to be higher than average (sometimes 14% or 15%) without being noticeable. So beware of false starts...

★ ★ ★ ★ ★

Greatest vintages of Rhone wines:

1911, 1923, 1929, 1945, 1961, 1978, 1998 and 2007.

Our selection

€

Costières de Nîmes - Domaine de Lognac - Cave de Pazac
Grape variety: Carignan, Syrah
Taste: Powerful, generous

€€

Saint-Joseph Cuvée Papy Stéphane Montez du Monteillet
Grape variety: Syrah
Taste: Fleshy, fruity

€€€

Châteauneuf-du-Pape Château de Beaucastel
Grape variety: Grenache, Mourvèdre, Syrah, Counoise, Cinsault
Taste: Powerful

Red wines and Rosés 80 %

White wines 20 %

4 500 000 hectoliters

57 000 hectares

Grape

Whites: Sauvignon, Sémillon, Muscadelle, Mauzac, Courbu, Petit Manseng, Gros Manseng.

Reds: Cabernet-Sauvignon, Cabernet franc, Merlot, Malbec, Tannat, Négrette, Fer Servadou.

Bergerac

Dordogne

Monbazillac

Cahors

Marcillac

Bordeaux

Gironde

Lot

Lot-et-Garonne

Aveyron

Landes

Tarn-et-Garonne

Gers

Tarn

Côtes de Millau

Bayonne

Toulouse

Irouléguy

Tarbes

Ariège

Jurançon

Madiran

The vineyards of the South-West are very extensive, stretching from the Basque Country to the Aveyron. In this region, which is particularly well known for its generous gastronomy (foie gras, cassoulet, pot-au-feu), the wines produced here are busy competing with the Bordeaux vineyards further north. One finds sweet white wines such as Monbazillac which remains very cheap and exceptional Madiran red wines.

Very good deals can be found in this traditional region. Reasonable price does not always mean bad quality!

Way of Santiago de Compostela

Vineyards of Irouléguy

The vineyards of the South-West are linked by the roads of Santiago de Compostela. This historical route has shaped this wine territory by spreading grape varieties from the Pyrenees (carried by the pilgrims). We also find values of the South-West common to all the cultural identities that make up this vast territory (Basque, Bearn, Landes, Gascon, Aveyron...).

★ ★ ★ ★ ★

Greatest vintages of South-West wines:

1985, 1987 and 1998.

Our selection

€
Côtes de Gascogne
Domaine Uby
Grape variety: Gros Manseng, Petit Manseng
Taste : Sweet, syrupy

€€
Domaine de Galouchey
Domaine Tariquet
Grape variety: Petit Manseng
Taste: Sweet, syrupy

€€€
Cahors – Le Cèdre
Château du Cèdre
Grape variety: Malbec
Taste: Powerful

The main French grape varieties correspond to the different grape species grown in France to make wine. These can sometimes be combined, and greatly influence the wine, its taste and character.

In France, there are more than 200 grape varieties authorized for production. However, 9 of them represent more than 65% of the cultivated surface. We will study these 6 black grape varieties and 3 white grape varieties that contribute to the viticultural greatness of France.

Grape variety	Description	Aromas			Location

Ugni Blanc

It is the main French grape variety used to make white wine. Originally from Italy, this variety has a large bunch and small to medium-sized fruits.
However, it should be used in blends to bring freshness.

Fruits	Flowers	Others
Lemon	Chamomile	Pine resin
Lime	Dill	Quince paste
Quince	Linden	Jam
Peach		

Sauvignon Blanc

Originally from the South-West, it then spread to France.It is characterized by a small cluster and small fruits. It is mainly used in the production of dry white wines but requires a lot of expertise to be cultivated. The wines it produces can be incredible and suitable for aging.

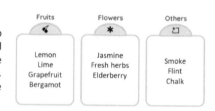

Fruits	Flowers	Others
Lemon	Jasmine	Smoke
Lime	Fresh herbs	Flint
Grapefruit	Elderberry	Chalk
Bergamot		

Chardonnay

Widely used in France and around the world, Chardonnay comes from Burgundy and is characterized by a small bunch and small fruits. It is one of the most famous grape varieties in the world, because of its adaptability and the wines it produces.

Fruits	Flowers	Others
Lemon	Linden	Butter
Lime	Acacia	Hazelnut
Apple	Honeysuckle	Brioche
Almond	Verbena	Vanilla
Pear	Honey	Toasted bread

Merlot

Merlot is the most widely used grape variety in France for making red wine. It is characterized by a medium-sized bunch and berries. Its particularly thick skin produces very good structured wines and when used with precision, it can produce very good wines for aging.

Fruits		While aging
Prune Blackberry Blueberry Black cherry Violet Mint	-	Leather Game Meat juice

Grenache noir

Grenache noir is characterized, as for Merlot, by a bunch and berries of medium size. Originally from Spain, it has gradually spread throughout France, producing fleshy wines. It is the main grape variety in the famous Châteauneuf-du-Pape.

Fruits	With the	While aging
Fig Strawberry Blueberry Garrigue Cocoa Cinnamon	Vanilla Coffee Liquorice Caramel	Dry fig Prune Mocha Leather

Carignan

Also originating from Spain, Carignan was imported by the pilgrims returning from Santiago de Compostela. The tannin is more limited for this variety, producing lighter red wines. It should be noted that very good wines for ageing are made from Carignan.

Fruits		Others

Blackberry Banana Prune	-	Garrigue Liquorice Flint

Cabernet Sauvignon

Cabernet Sauvignon is distinguished by the small size of its bunch and berries. Difficult to cultivate, it is particularly used in Bordeaux wines. Although tannic, it is nevertheless recognized for its particularly pleasant aromatic palette.

Fruits	With the barrel	While aging
Blackcurrant Blackberry Fern Pepper Jasmine Sandalwood	Oak Vanilla Clove Liquorice	Leather Tobacco Game Cedar Truffle

Pinot noir

Originally from Burgundy, Pinot noir is characterized by a small bunch and berries. Its low tannin character allows it to produce light and fruity wines. Many exceptional wines have been produced from this grape variety, which has been a staple of French wine history.

Fruits	With the barrel	While aging
Cheeey Raspberry Strawberry Blackcurrant Iris	Wood Vanilla Cinnamon Tobacco	Fur Leather Undergrowth Truffle Musk

Syrah

Syrah is characterized by a medium-sized bunch and berries. It does not withstand droughts because of its fragility, and produces dark-colored, rather full-bodied red wines with a high alcohol content. Syrah is also used for fruity and fine rosé wines.

Fruits	With the barrel	While aging
Blackberry Black cherry Blackcurrant Black pepper Nutmeg Chocolate	Cinnamon Coffee Smoke	Game Fig Tobacco Truffle

The perfect pairing

The oven is already preheating and you are looking for the perfect bottle to accompany your dish and delight your guests? You will find below a non-exhaustive list of perfect matches. These are only our recommendations, you are free to find other more daring ones!

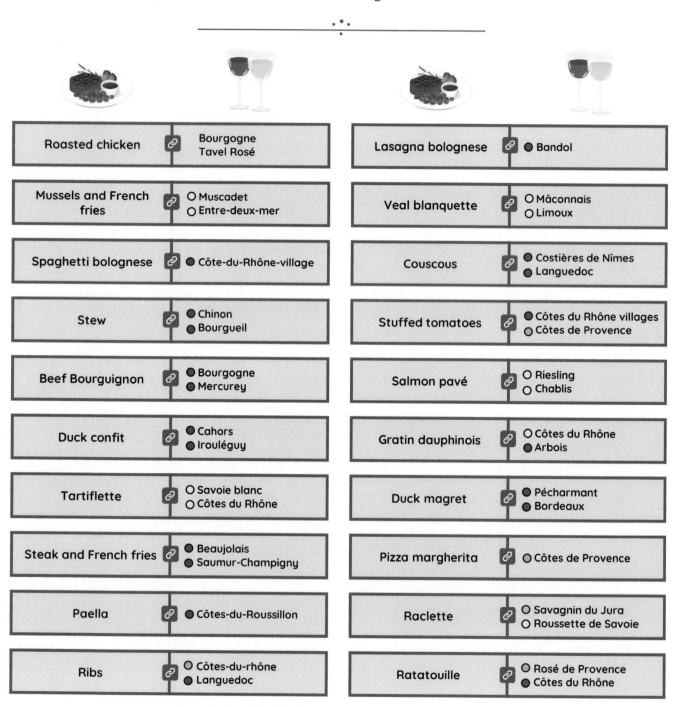

Roasted chicken	Bourgogne / Tavel Rosé
Mussels and French fries	○ Muscadet / ○ Entre-deux-mer
Spaghetti bolognese	● Côte-du-Rhône-village
Stew	● Chinon / ● Bourgueil
Beef Bourguignon	● Bourgogne / ● Mercurey
Duck confit	● Cahors / ● Irouléguy
Tartiflette	○ Savoie blanc / ○ Côtes du Rhône
Steak and French fries	● Beaujolais / ● Saumur-Champigny
Paella	● Côtes-du-Roussillon
Ribs	○ Côtes-du-rhône / ● Languedoc

Lasagna bolognese	● Bandol
Veal blanquette	○ Mâconnais / ○ Limoux
Couscous	● Costières de Nîmes / ● Languedoc
Stuffed tomatoes	● Côtes du Rhône villages / ○ Côtes de Provence
Salmon pavé	○ Riesling / ○ Chablis
Gratin dauphinois	○ Côtes du Rhône / ● Arbois
Duck magret	● Pécharmant / ● Bordeaux
Pizza margherita	○ Côtes de Provence
Raclette	○ Savagnin du Jura / ○ Roussette de Savoie
Ratatouille	○ Rosé de Provence / ● Côtes du Rhône

Shepherd's pie	🔗	● Sancerre rouge ● Beaujolais
Fondue Bourguignonne	🔗	● Bourgogne
Veal escalope à la milanaise	🔗	● Chinon ● Saint Nicolas Bourgueil
Chicken curry	🔗	○ Yellow wine ○ Condrieu
Pork tenderloin	🔗	● Saint Emilion ● Pomerol
Bouillabaisse	🔗	○ Bandol rosé ○ Provence blanc
Andouillette	🔗	○ Chablis ○ Givry
Hamburger	🔗	● Pic-saint-loup ● Saint-Joseph
Pasta and ham	🔗	● Beaujolais ● Gamay de la Loire
Snails with garlic	🔗	○ Mâcon blanc ○ Bourgogne aligoté
Camembert	🔗	● Gamay du Beaujolais ● Pinot noir de Bourgogne
Ossau-iraty, Cantal et le Saint-Nectaire	🔗	● Côtes-du-Rhône ● Côtes-de-Provence
Reblochon	🔗	○ Gewürstraminer Alsace
Pasta carbonara	🔗	○ Sauvignon ○ Pinot gris
Sauerkraut	🔗	○ Pinot blanc ○ Riesling
Lamb tagine	🔗	● Coteaux du Languedoc
Galette bretonne (crêpes)	🔗	○ Crément ○ Rosé d'Anjou
Sushis	🔗	○ Sauvignon ○ Sancerre rosé
Beef tartar	🔗	● Morgon ● Vacqueyras
Duck foie gras	🔗	○ Pinot gris ○ Jurançon Moelleux
Croque monsieur (sandwich)	🔗	● Beaujolais ○ Chardonnay
Omelette	🔗	○ Jasnières ○ Anjou
Mushroom risotto	🔗	○ Chablis grand cru ○ Côte de Beaune
Goat cheese	🔗	○ Sauvignon de la Loire ○ Chardonnay Bourgogne
Emmental and Comté cheese	🔗	○ Jura yellow wine ○ Grenache Languedoc
Roquefort cheese	🔗	● Banuyls ● Maury

Printed in Great Britain
by Amazon

78424663R00025